Tapping

Emotional Freedom Technique

Paul Ardennes

Copyright © 2015 and after - Univergy, LLC

ASIN: B01BGKG308

All rights reserved. No part of this publication may be reproduced, distributed, or transmitted in any form or by any means, including photocopying, recording, or other electronic or mechanical methods, without the prior written permission of the publisher, except in the case of brief quotations embodied in critical reviews and certain other noncommercial uses permitted by copyright law.

Tap your Energy

In support of research

Medical DISCLAIMER – No advice is herein given - Always consult a specialist if in any doubt of using these techniques.

You must not rely on the information in the series as an alternative to medical advice from your doctor or other professional healthcare provider

POWER HEALING SERIES I

Table of Contents

POWER HEALING SERIES I

Introduction

Why You Should Read This Book

Chapter 1. EFT 101 – the foundations of Tapping

Chapter 2. Why EFT Tapping works

Chapter 3. Affirmations and tapping

Chapter 4. Keep This In Mind Before You Start EFT tapping

Chapter 5. Practicing your affirmations

Chapter 6. EFT tapping in action (a guided tapping practice)

Chapter 7. EFT obstacles

Chapter 8. Taking EFT tapping a step further (customizing your tapping)

Chapter 9. Taking EFT tapping on the go

Chapter 10. Life lessons from tapping

About The Author

Books By Paul Ardennes

Introduction

The stresses of the modern world can bring you many ailments. However, while doctors and drugs primarily take care of the physical aspect; they can only do so much. Most of these are hardly able to completely heal the mind and the heart. That's why so many people remain broken even after having been pronounced healed by physicians.

Sometimes, people overlook the more important stuff. They failed to realize that no matter what medicines you take, what treatment you undergo, what diet you get yourself into, your body would never heal completely unless you free yourself from negative emotions.

Negative emotions are like poisons. They slowly eat you -- and through your body. The longer they stay inside you, the more powerful they become. How then, do you breakaway from these negative emotions?

Your body is more powerful than you think. It houses your mind and soul. It is the physical manifestation of your existence and most of all, it has the tremendous ability to heal itself.

You are an energetic being and inside your body is an energy that flows and brings you life. This energy is unstoppable. It has no limits and it cannot be extinguished.

You have the ability to tap into your body's incredible healing power. You simply need to learn where to tap and how to do it properly.

This book was written by someone who, like you, was once a prisoner of his negative emotions. Like you, he was also looking for ways to break free. He longed to heal himself and improve the quality of his life in the process. One day, he stumbled upon a healing method called Emotional Free Technique. After that, he never looked back. His life changed for the better and he has never been happier!

Why You Should Read This Book

This book will introduce you to the astonishing world of EFT. This technique is also more popularly referred to as Tapping. It is a universal method that is based on the premise that in order for all aspects of your life to improve, you must first let go of any unresolved emotional issues that might be standing in the way.

Dive into this book with an open mind and an open heart and allow yourself to discover the power you have within. Give yourself permission to see how strong you really are. Allow yourself to tap into the energy that is YOU!

Chapter 1. EFT 101 – The Foundations of Tapping

Emotional Freedom Technique or EFT tapping is considered as a form of psychological acupressure. It is anchored to the concept that emotional health is fundamental to achieve health and success in other aspects of your life. If your life is riddled with emotional barriers, you will never achieve your ideal health. You need to learn how to free yourself from these negative emotions and EFT Tapping can help you do that.

Acupuncture without the Needles

EFT Tapping operates along the same energy lines used in traditional acupuncture sans the invasive and terrifying needles. It uses pressure to stimulate the energies that dwell in these pressure points. All you need are your fingertips to do some simple tapping to help clear the circuits and enable the energy inside your body to flow freely.

About five thousand years ago, the Chinese discovered that inside the body lies a complex system of energy circuits called meridians. The energies that flow through these circuits are invisible to the naked eye but their effects are nonetheless very palpable. They can alter your mood and even change the way you think and feel.

In EFT, the combination of tapping the energy meridians and voicing positive affirmations were proven to be effective in clearing emotional blockages or short circuits in your body's energy system. Once these blockages are removed, you are able to restore balance between your body, mind and soul which all play a critical role in your quest to achieve optimum healing and health.

Location and Technique

Don't be fooled by the name. EFT may sound intimidating but the method is actually quite simple and easy to learn.

For EFT to be effective, there are two things that you must learn—where to tap and how to tap properly.

How to Tap

Before you begin, be sure to take off your watch and/or bracelet as well as your rings. These jewelries can interfere with the energy flow as you begin tapping.

Think of your fingertips as needle alternatives. You will be using them to apply pressure to the energy meridians in our body. Keep in mind though that there are also energy meridians found at the tip of your fingers.

You will be tapping with your index and middle fingers. You can use one hand or both (it doesn't really matter which hand (left or right). You can even switch hands while tapping. Or use both hands to cover more area.

When tapping, it is advisable that you use your fingertips and not your finger pads. Your fingertips contain more meridian points hence, you are able to stimulate more energy through them. If you have long fingernails however, then use of finger pads is permitted.

Tap solidly but gently. The pressure should be hard enough to stimulate the energy points but soft enough not to cause any bruising and scratches on yourself.

The actual number of times required for you to tap is not critical but to achieve optimum benefits, the number of tapping must be within one full breath (this usually will take about five to seven taps).

The beauty about EFT is that there is no prescribed sequence. You can tap the different energy points in any sequence and order. All you need to do is make sure that all points are covered. Most times, a simple top to bottom, bottom to top sequence will do to ensure that all energy medians are covered during tapping.

WHERE TO TAP

Knowing where to tap is quite easy. Each tapping point is right below the one before it so memorizing their locations will not be too difficult. The tapping points are often represented by abbreviations to easily commit them to memory:

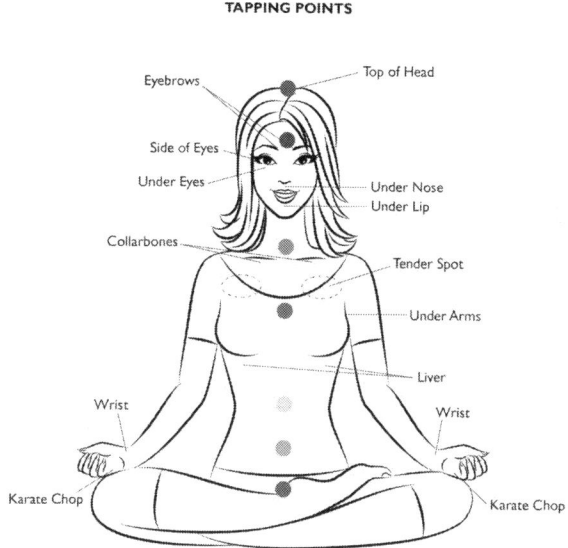

Photo from www.lornahollinger.com

1. TH (top of the head). This is the crown of your head. To stimulate the energy points here, bring your fingers to the center of your skull.
2. EB (eyebrow). These are the points right above the nose and your brows.
3. SE (side of the eye). These are located on the bone that frames the outside corner of your eyes.

4. UE (under the eye). These points are found right on the bones beneath your eyes and top of your cheekbones.
5. UN (under the nose). This is the region at the bottom of your nose and right above your upper lip.
6. Ch (chin). This energy point is not really located directly on the chin but rather on the space between your chin point and your lower lip.
7. CB (collar bone). The energy points runs from the breastbone or sternum all the way to the collar bone.
8. UA (under the arm). The energy points here are found about four inches below the armpit.
9. WR (wrists). The final energy points are found on the wrists.
10. KC (karate chop). This is the point at the side of your hands. It is named as such because touching or tapping these points will make you look like you are doing a karate move.

Chapter 2. Why EFT Tapping works

When you experience and go through a negative emotional state in your life, your brain goes into a state of alertness. It senses the negative emotion as a threat to your welfare and as a result, it prepares your body to go on either fight or flight mode.

As your body goes on alert, it pumps your bloodstream with fighting hormones like adrenaline to prepare you for the battle. Your body needs all the energy it can get to make sure that you survive the fight. Your muscle tension increases as your blood pressure, heart rate, blood sugar and breathing shoot up. Such response is instinctive. It is a primal instinct that has ensured the ancient man's survival amidst unforgiving preys and unpredictable forces of nature.

However, a lot of time has passed and the world has changed. The wild animals have already been caged. There is now weather forecasting technology to ensure that you are prepared for disasters. Physical threats have been eliminated and been replaced with emotional stress.

Painful experiences, unfounded worries and anxieties, loneliness, depression and hopelessness are the new threats to your existence. They are what plague the world of the modern man. And unlike the physical threats, they are much harder to eliminate.

Emotional stress is often rooted on traumatic experiences that can go way back to childhood. Sometimes you forget but more often than not, these negative memories surface from time to time when triggered. And once they surface, they also trigger the same bodily response towards stress.

The main switch to all these bodily response towards threats is the amygdala, a part of your body's limbic system. The limbic system houses your emotions and memories (whether they are positive or negative). When the amygdale senses a threat, it alerts the brain to go on a fight or flight mode and cycle begins.

Tapping puts a stop to the fight or flight response and reprograms the body to react in much calmer way. By tapping in the endpoints of the energy meridians, the amygdala's switch is turned off. It stops sending alarm to the brain that a threat is heading its way. Rather, it sends a calming message to the brain that all is safe and that it can finally relax now.

Studies done at Harvard Medical School can verify these claims. In the last decade, researchers discovered that the brain's stress response is lessened when the meridian points are stimulated by applying just enough pressure on them.

At first, the study was only focused on the benefits of acupuncture. However, follow up studies showed that even without the needles, the body's median points can still be stimulated by simply applying a tapping pressure on their end points. Such action also elicits the same healing results!

Chapter 3. Affirmations and Tapping

EFT tapping alone is effective enough but using it with affirmation statements makes it more potent in stimulating the energy points and promoting healing. Affirmations help address the emotional aspect of the illness.

Affirmations 101

Below is a traditional EFT affirmation phrase that you can use as you perform mechanical tapping:

- "Even though I have this _____, I deeply and completely accept/love myself."

It's up to you to fill out the blank field with whatever negative emotion that you are dealing with. It can be an addiction, an issue or a problem.

The goal of the phrase is to help you accept and acknowledge your present situation and in the process, accept yourself. Affirmations help you recognize what you've got here and now. They help you confront your fears and apprehensions and then remind you that no matter how ugly or bleak the situation may be, there is hope. Affirmations remind you not to be so hard on yourself. They remind you to be kinder, more loving and more forgiving of yourself.

You may not believe in the affirmation right away and that's okay. Your beliefs and values were not formed overnight. They were the results of years and years of life experiences. Continue reciting your affirmations while doing mechanical tapping. Reciting the affirmation over and over again helps change your perspective. Your mind is more pliable than you think. If given the same message over and over again, it begins to follow the "shape" and "form" of that message.

Therefore, even if you don't believe it, say it. If possible, say it out loud. Say it over and over again and eventually, your mind and heart will follow.

When you focus on the tapping and the affirmations alone, you tune out your problems, fears and apprehensions. All you've got are the repetitive tapping motions and words of affirmations. They become your sole focus and the rest (the negative emotions) simply fades away.

SOME TIPS TO HELP WITH YOUR AFFIRMATION PRACTICE

Here are some helpful tips to ease you into the practice. You can use these pointers when doing affirmations together with tapping to maximize their benefits to your health:

WHEN IN DOUBT…

Fears, doubts, apprehensions and other negative energies may come sneaking in while you are doing your tapping and affirmations. And they will. It's normal for you to feel all emotions. You are human after all and these emotions are part of you. But when they do come knocking, don't give them power over you. Don't run away from them. Don't deny their presence either.

Acknowledge the negative emotions that are running through your mind. Don't be afraid and ashamed to feel them. You can even incorporate them in your affirmations. You can say "even though I am afraid of (state what you are afraid of), I deeply accept/love myself."

Acknowledging the negative emotions will help you confront your present moment. This will help you realize that no matter where you are at now, at this point in your life, you are right where you should be—at the right time and doing the right thing.

It is this awareness of the present moment that can free you from the emotional chains that are holding you back. With acceptance comes understanding and once you understand why they are there, you are able to let go.

After acknowledging the negative emotions, go back to your affirmations.

PATIENCE IS A VIRTUE
The reason that some people think that affirmations don't work is because they lack patience. They think that change will happen after one round or a few days of tapping and affirmations. This is not always the case. Yes, there are some who experience change almost right away but there are also those who needed some time before they experience change in their lives.

The point here is simple; each person is different—physically, mentally and emotionally. Each one goes through life at his own pace and when the time is right, change will happen to him.

THE PRESENT MOMENT
Keep in mind that there is no other time but today so always say your affirmations in the present tense. The past is over and future may not even come. Seize the moment. Claim that whatever it is that you are asking for will happen today.

If you phrase your affirmations in future tense, your subconscious mind might literally place it in the future which. This can be a disadvantage for you as it might foresee your affirmations not happening until several years have passed.

Don't delay your goals, dreams and intentions. Don't let your mind delay you. Bring everything to the present moment for this, here, right now, is all that you've got.

LOVE IS ALL THERE IS

Affirmations play a vital role in making EFT tapping work. Saying that you love and accept yourself however can be difficult if you don't feel love for yourself.

Lack of self-love is the reason that there are so many emotional blockages in your life that prevent you from healing yourself. No amount of mechanical tapping and affirmations can completely remove them if you don't feel love for yourself.

Don't be too hard on yourself. Keep in mind that you are your best ally. When you criticize yourself, you add up to the emotional blockage in your life. You become what you think. You may not be able to control the emotions that are flooding your heart but remember that you have total control over your thoughts. Therefore, be mindful and selective of the thoughts that you allow to run through your mind. Choose those that nurture loving feelings towards yourself. Don't be your own worst critic. Befriend yourself and for once, cut yourself some slack.

FORGIVENESS IS THE KEY

Another key to successful EFT practice is forgiveness. This however can also be one of the most difficult aspects of emotional freedom.

Forgiveness should be a two-way street. You must be able to forgive others and at the same time, you must also be able to forgive yourself.

Choosing not to forgive others for the wrongs they've done to you will only wreck your emotional balance, not theirs. It is you who will end up feeling hurt. It is you who will feel the resentment and hate. And in the end, you continue to allow them to hurt you.

When you choose to forgive others, you also choose to let go of the negative emotions that are weighing you down. A heavy burden is suddenly lifted and you open yourself up to the possibility of receiving love and positive energy in return.

Forgiving also enables you to let go of the past and remain engaged in the present moment. Holding a grudge forces to look back and dwell on the bad times. Forgiving gives you permission to lay the past to rest in order for you to live in the present moment. For it is only in the present moment that you are able to nurture and heal yourself and prepare for a healthier and more promising future.

SELF-TALK MATTERS

Your words are powerful so be careful with the words that you are telling yourself. They can make or break you.

Talking to yourself is not weird at all. Self-talk is what shapes your thoughts, your perception of the world and in the end, your reality. The words that come out of your mouth are extensions of who you truly are. If your self-talk is focused on what's bad and what's not right, the words that will come out of your mouth will be full of negative energy.

Energies are contagious. If you are emitting nothing but negativity, you will likely attract the same kind of energy. This adds up to the blockages that are short circuiting your energy medians. EFT tapping can help unblock that but you must also have with you reinforcements such as positive self-talk or affirmations.

For EFT to become more effective, you must approach this technique from a place of and acceptance. You must understand that you want to change not because you are bad or there is something wrong with you but because you want uncover the best version of you. You accept and understand that you are a good person and that are full of possibilities. What you seek, you already have. What you want to achieve, you already are. All you need to do is tap into these possibilities by getting rid of your emotional blockages.

Chapter 4. Keep This In Mind Before You Start EFT tapping

EFT tapping can bring your life tremendous relief and benefits if used properly. It teaches you how to heal yourself by getting rid of the negative energies that are blocking your energy medians. It teaches how to tap into the power that you already have within. This chapter will show you the crucial things to watch out for when going through your EFT practice to ensure that you are using the techniques properly and effectively:

Strength in numbers

Some people complain that they don't find EFT effective when they are performing it by themselves. This usually happens if the person doing the EFT is new and is still trying to learn the ropes of optimizing his or her energy output. If you feel that your energy is not strong enough to remove emotional blockages, feel free to look for others who can share their energies with you as you continue your EFT practice. It can be a friend who also does EFT tapping, or even a therapist.

Energies can be multiplied and combined with others who vibrate in the same frequency as yours. Thus it is important that you seek out people who are within your tribe. They are the people who share the same dreams and beliefs that you do. They are the people who remind you of who and what you want to achieve. They are the people who will support you and not criticize you. They are your energy allies.

A change in perspective

Energies are fluid therefore it is important that you are mindful of the cognitive shifts that can occur during tapping. You will know that a cognitive shift has transpired when you suddenly see a problem or issue in a different light. Such changes in perspective can lead you to new pathways towards healing.

Don't let a cognitive shift go unnoticed. These subtle changes in your perception will offer you clues regarding the root cause of your problems. Give yourself permission to stop after a few rounds of tapping and check in with yourself. Notice if you feel anything different. Be mindful of new feelings that might have surfaced. Go back to your problem or issue that you are trying to resolve and notice if there is any change in the way you see it and your feelings towards it.

IT PAYS TO BE SPECIFIC

The success of EFT relies on two things – tapping and affirmations. Both must be performed correctly in order for you to achieve ideal healing.

The words that you used during affirmations must be specific to your goal. They must clearly define what you want to happen and what you want to accomplish during the practice. Keep in mind that the affirmations that you say to yourself over and over again during tapping are messages that you are sending out to the universe. They carry with them your intentions. They carry with them your energy. And whatever it is that you put out there, you also attract in return.

FOCUS AND TUNE IN

It is normal for you to become distracted while tapping. Unwanted thoughts may begin to run through your mind. Feelings may begin to surface. You mind might begin to wander in the past or it might try to peek into the future. You might start to feel different emotions stirring as you become more engaged in the present moment. When they happen (as they will), don't panic. Don't reprimand yourself for having those thoughts and feelings. It's okay for you to think and feel them.

Give yourself permission to acknowledge and accept what just happened and then slowly allow yourself to go back to your affirmations. They will serve as your anchor to the present moment. They will remind you of your intentions. They will remind you that there is no place and time that you'd rather be but here, right now.

IT IS ALL YOU, BABY

Healing happens through you! Whether you are practicing with a therapist or a friend, keep in mind that you are the only person responsible for your own healing. It is your energy that is flowing through you. You have full control over your thoughts. You dictate the flow of energy in your body. No one else is responsible for your healing but you. Other people might believe in you but all of these will not have any effects on you if you, yourself will not believe in your own strength.

Your affirmations should be about you. Work on your emotional issues. Forget what others think and feel. What matters at this point, is you.

Hydrate!

Believe it or not but water is essential to ensure that you have a successful EFT practice. Water is a conductor of electricity. Electricity is energy and EFT accesses the energy that flows through you. The ideal amount is about one quart of water per day for every fifty pounds body weight.

Chapter 5. Practicing your affirmations

Giving yourself affirmations may seem an easy feat at first glance. But once you get into it, you might actually be surprised how challenging it is sometimes to say something nice about yourself. Oftentimes, certain emotional issues can prevent you from opening up to this experience (these will be discussed in detail in Chapter 7). You got used to the habit of criticizing yourself far too many times that you forgot what it's like to say something good about you.

For most of your life, you probably encountered people telling you to do this and that because you weren't good enough. They tell you to be this person because what you are now does not make the cut. You hear these things over and over again that at the end of the day, you end up telling yourself the same thing. In your quest to fit in and be loved, you became your own worst critic.

This chapter will help you practice your affirmations. This form of positive self-talk can help reprogram your mind's perception of you! Below are some pointers that you can practice to make your affirmations more effective:

Say it first, the rest will follow

You might find it difficult at first to believe your affirmations. And that's okay. You don't have to believe in it right away. Keep in mind that you are trying to unlearn many years of negative self-talk. Such things can be difficult to forget.

But beliefs are just like habits. By bombarding your brain with a specific affirmation, you begin to create a new path in your mind -- one that is aligned to the version of you that you wish to achieve. Soon, your brain begins to catch up and begins to send the same signal all over your body.

As you go through your affirmations, you must keep in mind one crucial thing—affirmations are not lies. They are declarations of who you truly are. The true you that has been buried beneath layers of self-doubt, low self-esteem and negative thinking. Affirmations remind you of who you once were. They remind you of the person that you chose to forget a long time ago in exchange for other people's acceptance.

Timing is everything

Commitment is about making time. Setting a time of your day to practice EFT tapping and your affirmations can help reinforce the habit in your daily life.

In actuality, you can practice tapping, anytime and anywhere. For beginners however, it is encouraged that you establish a routine during your first few months to establish the habit.

Mornings, upon waking up, are always the best time to begin your tapping practice. Everything is still fresh. The day has just begun and you have the opportunity right at your fingertips to determine what kind of day you will have.

Before going to sleep is also another good time to practice EFT tapping. When all is said and done, you'd want to end your day with affirmations that you can carry with your subconscious while you sleep. The tapping mechanism can also help relax tensed and clogged up meridian points.

If you are the type of person who prays before going to sleep, you can incorporate tapping as you say your prayers. They are also in a way, a form of affirmation. They remind you of what is good and happy. They remind you of all you can possibly be.

Mirror talk

Talk to yourself in front of a mirror actually helps. It might look silly and downright crazy but practicing in front of a mirror will help improve your affirmations.

During your first few tapping sessions, try to do it while staring at yourself, in the mirror. Particularly, look into your eyes. Doing this somehow creates a deeper connection between your conscious mind and your subconscious mind. The mirrors also act as reflectors. They bounce back to you all the positive energies that you are sending out into your surroundings.

Oftentimes, you don't believe the affirmations that you are telling yourself because you spent most of your time beating yourself up. You were always too hard on yourself. You've set high expectations that you feel you must achieve so you don't feel like a failure. You are not used to cutting yourself some slack and telling yourself that it's okay to slow down and just let things be.

Looking into your eyes, in front of the mirror, allows you to have a conversation with yourself. You allow yourself to see the true you that for the longest time has been trying to break free. You allow your message to reach the rightful receiver—YOU!

Chapter 6. EFT Tapping in Action (A Guided Tapping Practice)

Now that you have a deeper understanding of the factors and forces at play during EFT, it is high time that you put what you've learned into practice. This chapter will show you how to go through one round of EFT tapping. Think of it as some sort of a guided meditation. It will walk you through each step from beginning to end:

1. Begin by looking for a place where you would feel relaxed and at ease.
2. Find a seat that is comfortable for you. You can sit on the floor or on a chair. If you'd rather do it standing, that's also okay. The point is, you arrive into a pose that is comfortable for you.
3. Once settled, begin to calm yourself by focusing on your breath. Allow it to steady your heartbeat and relax your muscles. Focus on the rise and fall of your chest. Try to follow your breath from beginning to end—from the moment you inhale until the time that you exhale. Go through this over and over again until you find your pace and allow your breath to take you to a more calm and relaxed state.
4. Set your intention by focusing on a problem that you'd like to work on. When trying to identify the emotional issue that you'd like to work on, you need to come from a place of honesty and acceptance. Don't work on an issue just because others told you to do so. Work on an issue that you feel is holding you back. Don't be ashamed of your fears and your emotions.
5. Tune in to your problem by actually allowing it to occupy your thoughts. That's right. You need to confront your issues head on. Often times, you spend your time running away from them. During EFT, you left with no choice but to face them with a certain openness and softness. You need to acknowledge them without fear and judgment.

6. Once you've identified your issue, select an appropriate affirmation. Use the traditional EFT phrase "even though I have this _____, I deeply and completely love/accept myself."
7. Begin to recite this phrase over and over again. State your affirmations with passion, conviction, certainty and enthusiasm. If you are not comfortable reciting your affirmations out loud, you can keep your voice's normal tone and phase. What matters in the end is the passion, energy and commitment that you put into it every time you say it.
8. Once you've gotten into the rhythm of your affirmations, gently place your fingertips on the crown of your head. At this point, it's up to you to decide whether you'd use one or both hands for tapping. For beginners, it is advisable that you begin with both hands.
9. Lightly begin to tap on the crown of your head and begin to recite your affirmations. Begin to increase the pressure as you see fit but be careful not to bruise your skin. Tap about five to seven times within one breath cycle. Once done, move on to median spot number 2 (as shown in the diagram on chapter 1).
10. Continue tapping while reciting your affirmations, from one point to the next until you reach the last median spot. If in any case you felt that a particular energy median needs more stimulation, feel to go back to it and increase the frequency and length of your taping.
11. All throughout your tapping exercise be mindful of your affirmations. Make sure that you continue to recite them while tapping.
12. Once you've reached the end of the median points, begin to slow down the frequency and intensity of your tapping until it comes to a halt.
13. Notice how you feel after and allow yourself to relish in it.

This guided tapping exercise is simply a guide to get you started. Follow this to ease yourself into the technique. Once you gotten the hang of it, feel free to veer off the beaten path by staying longer on a certain median point that needs tending. Just don't forget the anchor that holds it all together—your affirmations.

Chapter 7. EFT Obstacles

Sometimes, no matter how much you want to reverse a negative emotion through affirmations, there are moments when you just can't seem to make it work. You were tapping on all the right places and saying the right words but nothing is happening.

There are certain subconscious mechanisms going on inside you that you might not be aware of. These mechanisms can block your abilities to heal yourself. Below are some of the most common blockages that can hind EFT healing:

Doubt

Doubt in your ability to heal yourself can greatly impact the flow of energy in your body. When you doubt yourself, you end up putting on the brakes on whatever reversal process you might have set in motion when you began tapping. Doubt weakens your faith in your strength to overcome your fears and apprehensions. It makes you second-guess your ability to move on from your painful memories. It makes you weak and fragile.

Doubt is like acid that slowly eats you up from the inside. Just a shred of it is enough to weaken the foundations of your beliefs. It is enough to make you question every decision you've made and you plan on making. It can even make you question the reasons you decided to try EFT tapping. It leaves you feeling unmotivated and hopeless.

Denial

Denying that you need healing is another blockage that is common during EFT tapping. Most people don't think that they need help until it's too late. They keep on telling themselves that they're okay when really, they are slowly crumbling down from the inside.

When you are in denial, you run away from the roots of your emotional issues. You end up blocking your energy medians so no matter how much tapping you do to stimulate them, you end up with the same feeling of being stuck and unworthy.

Safety

Venturing into something you're not familiar with can be scary sometimes. The fear of things going wrong and compromising your safety can be very daunting. This can make you want to run and hide. It can even paralyze and stop you dead on your tracks.

When you don't feel safe, you stop trusting in your ability to care for yourself. You are unable to let go of your apprehensions. You stop yourself from surrendering to the experience that the present moment has to offer. In your fear of getting hurt, you end up insulating yourself from the benefits that tapping can bring to your life. You stop the energies from flowing freely into your body. You don't allow the healing to take place.

Ego

This is probably the biggest obstacle of them all. Oftentimes, pride gets in the way of things. You felt that you know everything. You felt that you've got it all figured out. Truth is, you don't. But then again, you are too proud to ask for help. You are too proud to notice the signs. So you ignore them and try to do things your way, not knowing that you are actually going the wrong way.

Ego can also make you feel entitled. You become so full of yourself that begin to believe that you deserve to get what you want, right away. This line of thinking can cause restlessness and impatience which return, screw up the harmonious flow of energy inside your body.

The underdog syndrome

Some people don't receive healing because they believe that they don't deserve healing. They see feel that they deserve the pain and suffering that they are going through. They feel guilty for wanting to get better. This is particularly common with patients who have gone through a traumatic experience. Such resistance can be very difficult to overcome and may require additional psychological help.

The feeling unworthiness can propel a person to push away the good things that might be coming his way. No amount of affirmations can make him change his mind about accepting that good things that he actually deserves.

Chapter 8. Taking EFT tapping a step further (customizing your tapping)

Following the guided EFT tapping practice, learning the basic set up and reminder phrases can be very helpful especially if you are a beginner. However, as days pass by and you become accustomed to the flow, your mind and body will begin to yearn for something more natural and organic.

Customizing your tapping practice can optimize the benefits that it brings to your mind and body. You are able to adjust the intensity and frequency of tapping according to your needs. You are able to personalize the scripts to cater to areas in your life that need the most help.

In this chapter, you will learn how to take your EFT tapping a step further by becoming more specific. You will learn tips on how to tailor fit your affirmations to your needs.

The extended set up phrase and Tell the Story Technique – Level 1

This set up will help you describe your problem in detail. It will target the root cause of the emotional issue more effectively. You will have a more personal experience from the practice.

Below is a sample flow that you can use as a guide as you free flow into your tapping practice:

- Begin by choosing a specific issue or problem that you want to address in your life.
- Once you are able to identify your focus area and you begin reciting the traditional phrase "Even though I have this

_____ ", fill in the blank with a description of the issue. Don't limit it to one word. Pretend that you are talking to a friend and you are confiding in her your problems. Pretend as if you are telling a story.
- Go over the description several times if you must until you feel that you have a detailed description of the problem.
- Don't forget to end the description with "I deeply and completely accept myself."
- As you recite your description, take note of certain keywords that will serve as your reminder phrases. To identify your key words, pay attention to the intensity of feelings that certain words can evoke from you. These words will excite you more than the rest. Reminder phrases will help you focused on the problem. They are extremely helpful when you are dealing with external and internal distractions.
- Go through one "round" with this setup. Describe what was happening to you at each energy median you tap on. Keep in mind that descriptions can include physical sensations, feelings and matter of fact details of the event that has transpired.
- Remember that it is not your goal to eliminate emotional blockages in just one round so, be patient.
- Repeat the same set up in the succeeding rounds and pay attention to the subtle changes in your mood.

THE EXTENDED SETUP PHRASE – LEVEL 2

Once you are comfortable doing the extended set up phrase, you are ready to flow into your tapping practice:

- Begin by going through the extend set up sequence. Incorporate 15-20 taps per sequence or median point.
- Again, don't forget to end the description with the phrase "I deeply and completely accept myself."

- Then, gradually, as you move on to the next energy point, add in another reminder phrase that may not be part of the original phrase. Don't overthink it. Just trust on whatever pops into your mind.
- Continue adding up new words and phrases as you move to the rest of the median points. Don't be shy to add whatever word or phrase that comes to mind. Adding more key words will help you zero in on the true nature of your problem.
- Below is an example of a Setup Reminder Combination:
    - KC - Even though my mother told me that I sing off key and I will never have it in me to sing in front of an audience, I deeply and completely accept myself. She told me that my voice is really bad in front of my classmates. I was completely embarrassed. I was about to cry. I was only seven years old then but I felt like my future was doomed. I felt hopeless. I felt like running away and crying all day. I was really uncomfortable because my friends were staring at me. I wish she never told me that. I deeply and completely accept myself anyway."
    - TOH She told me that my voice is really bad.
    - EB I was so completely embarrassed!
    - SE I felt like crying.
    - UE I felt hopeless.
    - UN and I felt like running away and crying all day.
    - Ch I was only seven years old then
    - CB but I felt like my future was doomed
    - UA I wish she never told me that
    - KC I deeply and completely accept myself anyway.

Keep in mind that you have the option to end on any point in the sequence. You only have to make sure that you complete one round or have gone through all of the points at least once. As you experiment with this free flowing form of tapping, remember to check for emotional intensity at every median point. Be mindful of the shift in emotions and overall sensation. They will help you decide whether the key words you've chosen are effective or not.

One thing you must remember as you deepen your EFT tapping practice is "freedom." The rule here is that, there are no rules! All these are mere guides the help you in your journey. You are free to venture to the less trodden path (in fact, that is recommended!). You have the permission to seek that which makes you feel good. And once you find it, go after it with all that you've got.

Chapter 9. Taking EFT tapping on the Go

Many people can attest to the positive effects that EFT tapping has brought into their lives. However, they are concerned about using EFT in public. Some felt that the motions involved in tapping will make them stand out of the crowd. They don't want to draw attention to themselves. They don't want to be embarrassed.

There are actually many ways that you can use EFT in public without be obvious. Below are some pointers and modifications that you can incorporate in your tapping practice to make it less conspicuous when you feel the need to do it in public:

- No touch. Dr. John Diepold developed a technique that doesn't involve tapping. This is called the 'Touch and Breathe" method instead of using the usual staccato way of tapping. This is a no fuss, easy technique that is subtle enough to be performed in public places.

    To do this, touch each median point but hold off on the tapping part. Hold your finger on a particular energy point long enough to recite your EFT phrase or affirmation. Once done, breathe in deeply then move on to the next spot. This method is not only subtle; it can also be very relaxing. The steady breathing can calm the body and soothe the mind. It can even bring you to a meditate state.

- Karate chop only. If you prefer to sensation of the tapping motion, then limit the tapping to the spot called Karate chop while pronouncing or thinking your EFT affirmations. Use this spot as a substitute to the other median spots.

    Visualize yourself moving on to the next median spot (even though your finger is still positioned over your Karate chop) and recite your affirmation. Picture your EFT sequence in your head and keep repeating your affirmations to yourself while continuously tapping on your Karate chop spot.

Since your Karate chop spot is situated in a concealed area of your body, your tapping won't be as obvious if you were doing it on your head and other visible body parts. This action is very subtle and can be performed almost under any circumstance. You can be sitting on your desk, attending a staff meeting or going on a date and still be able to tap on your energy points. You can simply keep your hands underneath the table and carry on with the conversation and they won't notice a single thing.

- Use your imagination. Believe in the power of your imagination. This option is called "mental EFT." Though not applicable to all, those who have good imagination can find this very effective and beneficial.

Mental EFT in a nutshell is performing EFT tapping in your head. Imagine your whole EFT tapping sequence from beginning until the end. Imagine your hands and fingertips on the crown of your head. Imagine them tapping on your TH (top of head) point. Recall the sensations that you feel whenever you tap on that spot and imagine yourself saying your affirmations.

This method is more effective if you are doing this in a relaxed state wherein your mind is clear, calm and still. Continuous practice of mental EFT can help you get rid of the clutter in your mind that normally distracts you from your day to day activities.

- Excuse yourself. If by any means, you are unable to do any of the three techniques mentioned above, then don't be shy to excuse yourself from the situation and find a private place to perform EFT tapping.

It's okay for you to step away from it all and give yourself the time that it deserves. There will be moments when your emotional intensity is too much that no amount of mental tapping or touch and breathe technique can subdue. At this point, you need the real thing and there is no shame in giving yourself permission to get away.

Find a place where you can be alone. Don't forget to find a place where you'll feel safe and comfortable. In here, go over your EFT sequence until you've toned down your emotional intensity. Once calm, you will be able to resume your activities normally.

Chapter 10. Life lessons from tapping

You can learn a lot from EFT tapping. Aside from the obvious physical and emotional benefits, this practice can also give you life lessons that you can take with you as go about your daily activities:

The power within

One of the greatest lessons that you will learn from EFT is that you have the power to heal yourself. Knowing that you have this ability will enable you to believe in the amazing and powerful person that you've always been. Tapping teaches you to turn the search for peace, happiness and healing inward. It teaches you to acknowledge and believe that you have everything that you need to make yourself a better person. You have the power to turn things around. All you need to do is tap into this power that dwells inside you.

Patience

Tapping also teaches you to be patient. Changes don't happen after one round of tapping. Some emotional blockages are difficult to eliminate especially if they've been there for quite some time. Your body has grown accustomed to their presence that it has begun to treat them as part of itself. Getting rid of these emotional blockages can take time. You need to allow the process to work at its own pace. EFT teaches you how to tend to yourself while tapping into your energy within.

Gratitude

When you go through your affirmations during tapping, you are reminded of the things that you already have. You are reminded that you don't have to look far to find healing and happiness in your life. EFT tapping will allow you to see that you have everything that you need right at this very moment. It teaches you to how to have a grateful heart.

Self-love

Your use of affirmations teaches you to accept and love yourself for what and who you truly are. It teaches you to be kinder, more compassionate and more forgiving of yourself. Affirmations will only work if they are coming from a place of acceptance and love. For you to have that, you need to learn to kind to yourself. You need to learn to appreciate yourself for your strengths and weaknesses.

EFT tapping teaches you one crucial lesson – that self-love is not selfish. You need to tend to yourself before you are able to give love to others. You need to forgive yourself first before you can forgive others. You can't light other people's paths if the light inside you is turned off.

About The Author

Paul is a senior researcher in Electronic Medicine at Medicollege. He is a Reiki Master in Usui and Seichim styles. He practices auricular therapy and neuromusicology as well as electronic medicine.

He is trained in Psychologies (psychoanalysis, general psychology and applied psychologies)

He writes fiction and non-fiction books. In his childhood, he had experiences that enabled him to develop, enhance and experiment with the abilities described in the series.

He studied acupuncture with the Beijing college of Acupuncture .

He treats people in Europe and Central America on a rotational basis and wherever he happens to be otherwise. His sessions are always free.

He is forming an Open Club University where people can participate to experiments and relate their own experiences to compare with other people and to use for surveys.

Books By Paul Ardennes

AWAKEN Series:

AWAKEN Your Auras – Series I – Book One

AWAKEN Your Chakras – Series I – Book Two

AWAKEN Your Third Eye – Series I – Book Three

AWAKEN Your Mind – Series I – Book Four

AWAKEN Your Self – Series I – Book Five

AWAKEN Your Knowledge – Series I – Book Six

Power Healing New Series –

Power Healing: EFT – Series II – Volume One

Power Healing: NLP – Series II – Volume Two

Power Healing: I-Ching and DNA – Series II – Volume Three

Power Thinking Series

Power Thinking: The Efficient Mind (Hemisphere dominance, Speed reading and Memorization techniques)

Play with your Creativity (His & Hers) - Series III –

- Personal (Finance, relationship, health, work)- Book One
- The Others (Friendship, Help, Team ('m vs U), Togetherness (U vs 'm)

ONE LAST THING...

I want to thank you once more for taking the time to download this book and taking another step towards your goal.

I really hope that I was able to help you find directions to Awaken The Powers Hidden In You. Remember that it takes time. *It took us millions of years to bury the powers. To dig them back out may take more than a few hours*. Do all the exercises and the activity plans that I designed uniquely for you. Some of them will bring results. The sum total will bear fruits.

Keep on practicing. And please don't forget to let me know how effective they are in your daily experiments, and what experiences you get with them. This will help me revise the books thanks to your personalized inputs.

If you enjoyed this book or found it useful I'd be very grateful if you'd post a short review on Amazon. Your support really does make a difference and I read all the reviews personally so I can get your feedback and make this book even better.

If you'd like to leave a review then all you need do is [click this link right now](#).

Thank you and enjoy this extra time spent with yourself.

Made in the USA
Las Vegas, NV
27 November 2022

60477172R00024